THE MORE DECEIVED

poems about love and lovers

Norman Schwenk

Distributed by:
Parthian Books
The Old Surgery
Napier Street
Cardigan SA43 1ED
Wales

Alley Press
2005

Published by:
Alley Press
13, Orchard Place
Cardiff CF11 9DY
Wales

ISBN 1-902638-65-4

Book design by RX.

Printed by Dalton Printers, Thesiger Street, Cathays, Cardiff

CONTENTS

Love Lies With Truth 7

A Mother Commits the Seven Deadly Sins in Five Minutes Flat 8

Near Today 9

Green Sedan 10

A Serious Lover 11

Separation 12

On the Famous Voyage 13

A Perfect Christmas Tree 14

Valentine 15

Waiting Room 16

Cupid's Sprite 17

Record 18

Song: Carrickfergus 19

Twins 21

Haunted 22

Llandaff Walk 23

Welsh Harpist 29

Demon 30

Thanksgiving 31

If Rossetti Read Dickinson 32

Nearness 33

Reluctant Dragon 34

Song: Rock On, Crimson Cavalier 35

VCR 36

Rime of St Melangell 37

Tin Man 40

Bosom Buddy 41

Poetry or Love 42

Christmas Toy 43

Miracle 44

The More Deceived 45

ACKNOWLEDGEMENTS

Acknowledgements are due the following magazines: *New Welsh Review, Poetry New York, Poetry Nottingham, Poetry Wales, Scintilla;* and the following anthologies: *Bard of the Year 1994* (Poetry Digest) *Versatility* (Tears In the Fence) *The So What? Factory* (Cardiff University) *The Hare That Hides Within* (Parthian Books).

Immeasureable help with these poems has been given me by my students, friends and colleagues. I would especially like to thank Tiffany Atkinson, Jane Blank, Karen Buckley, Lindsay Clarke, Anne Cluysenaar, Bryn Daniel, Deborah Davies, Ann Drysdale, Colin Evans, Roger Ellis, John Freeman, Danny Gorman, David Greenslade, Claire Keegan, Hilary Llewellyn-Williams, Steve Prescott, Jenny Sullivan and Jim Tucker.

I want to give particular thanks to Richard Cox for his generous assistance in preparing the design of this book. The maze pattern on the cover is imitated from the labyrinth on the floor of Chartres Cathedral.

Thanks to Sarah Maurice of Dalton Printers for her advice and assistance, to Rhian Evans for her proof reading, and to Hilary Charlesworth for her mole-trap story.

A Perfect Christmas Tree' refers to Walt Whitman's *Song of Myself* ; *On the Famous Voyage* is the title of a poem by Ben Jonson; `If Rossetti Read Dickinson' refers to several poems by Christina Rossetti, and also to Emily Dickinson's *One Need Not Be A Chamber To Be Haunted*. `The Rime of St Melangell' quotes Samuel Taylor Coleridge's *The Rime of the Ancient Mariner.* The references to *The Wizard of Oz* in `Tin Man' are more to the film than the book.

FOR DEBORAH

HAMLET: I loved you not.

OPHELIA: I was the more deceived.

LOVE LIES WITH TRUTH

Love tried to live with Truth.
God, she found it hard:
He ranted in his sleep,
Left rubbish in the yard.

She tried to live without him.
That was even worse:
Waking beside utter strangers,
Telling lies in verse.

Now they share a house.
They've got it about right:
He sees her nearly every day;
She visits him at night.

All their friends agree.
Solicitors concur:
She's aimless without him;
He's heartless without her.

A MOTHER COMMITS THE SEVEN DEADLY SINS IN FIVE MINUTES FLAT

Lying on the sofa,
Twiddling my remote—
Suddenly a yearning
For Christmas chocolate,

Even though it's August.
Breathless, I'm upstairs
Rifling the wardrobe,
Gorging gooey squares.

Now it's hubby calling
From his bubble bath,
`Something nice for you, dear!'
It's little pink giraffe.

Two long minutes later,
Stumbling down the stair,
I spy with my little eye
The neighbours' brand-new car.

Once I had a mini,
Now an overdraft—
A maxi one, with overdrive.
I make out it's a laugh.

All at once the children
Start a mammoth row.
Tiddly on the grapes of wrath,
I clip them round the ear.

An average day at our house—
Happy, normal fare.
Forgiveness is perpetual,
Sinners, don't despair!

NEAR TODAY

Yesterday, when you were far,
I felt you were so near.
Today, when you were close at hand,
You seemed not to be here.

Tonight, now you are far again,
And feel so far away,
I hope that, when tomorrow comes,
You will be near today.

GREEN SEDAN

Two lovers clasp, her lips on his,
Under a smiling moon.
A car careers into the lane
And almost cuts them down.

It's Jealousy, the Green Sedan,
Who envies their delight.
He lusts to see their blood on brick
Reflecting the moonlight.

True lovers have a dancing movement
Only they perform—
Nothing fancy, strictly ballroom—
For evading harm.

And so they dance, in dark Harm's Way,
Lightly skipping free
From Jealousy's relentless, raging,
Boring circuitry.

A SERIOUS LOVER

A Serious Lover felt a fancy
Undermine his soul,
Like a vast, velvet lawn succumbs
To a tiny, velvet mole.

He said, `I'll fetch my mole-trap
With its wicked spring and dart,
Expunge this roguish fancy,
So unworthy, from my heart.'

So he scoured shed and attic...
It was nowhere to be found.
At last he realised his trap
Must still be underground.

Metal-detector man strode forth:
His robot-waddle gait
Surveyed each centimetre
With magnetic-magic plate...

But still no bloody mole trap.
Where had the bastard gone?
He stopped to look. His raging eye
Beheld the ravaged lawn,

Dug up for coins and bottle-caps,
Five paperclips, one nail—
A hundred little black hills
And not one the mole-trap grail.

The mole soon strangely vanished.
And hanging from a hook
The trap turned up in his garage,
Where he'd forgot to look.

SEPARATION

What a relief to hear
You are in pain.
They spread an ugly rumour
That you were fine.

Why is it such a comfort
You are in Hell,
Like me, when all my heart
Wishes you well?

ON THE FAMOUS VOYAGE

When lovers face the facts of Hell
And voyage in a stinking ditch
With demons jeering from each bank,
And no hope of appeal...

They know at last they have each other,
Face to face, with oars and rudder—
They, and only they, must find
A smile behind the horror.

Then silently, as if the moon
Soared on the current of a cloud,
Their little skiff begins to lift
And leave the foul lagoon.

And now in oceans of blue eyes
They search for continents unknown,
Discover realms of inner space
Where galaxies can hide.

Their fragile, magic boat has proven
Seaworthy among the stars;
And inwardly they bless the Hell
That sped them to this Heaven.

A PERFECT CHRISTMAS TREE

I want to taste your blood again.
I want to suck my fingers
and taste the iron. I want my mouth
cupped upon your other mouth,
savouring the rich trickle, trickle...

Look, the shape of a tiny
Gothic steeple, a perfect Christmas tree,
your kissable lips, this warm,
delectable flesh, scalloped, fragrant.
Under my nails
your blood dries in sweet rust flakes.

Your flavour and aroma are nothing like
the mountain spring—tasteless,
odourless, colourless, for my mouth
forever—they are only for now,
this long, urgent moment,
when the tongue must take notice,
the instant the blood spurts.

VALENTINE

I listened to your heart today
Ka-thumping wonderous fast,
And prayed that it would go always,
And no beat would be last.

WAITING ROOM

In a hard world of transient hearts
his heart is like this waiting room:
a serviceable place to pause,
a little cold, even in summer,
a bit dingy, even when cleaned,
spare to the point of being stark;
mostly a place of silence, boredom,
but now and then good melodrama;
used by many, abused by some,
not a corridor, not a home,
empty, empty for nights on end,
and always, utterly, loved by none.

CUPID'S SPRITE

Has Cupid got some devilish Sprite,
Who, once he's done his bowman's job
And shot his bolt and skewered hearts
In one still-beating, joint kebab,

Busies herself between those hearts
And stirs the blood with impish glee:
That letter glides beneath the mat,
Straight down the sewer slips that key?

Do lovers need her meddling when
Mere loving is quite hard enough?
Putting some poor girl up the duff,
Just when the going is getting tough—

It beggars comprehension—why?
Does Cupid doubt that two-are-one
And seek to test his eagle eye,
Or is it sheer sadistic fun?

Though a mere Sprite, she does real harm.
And what can hapless lovers do?
Except the one thing sprites eschew,
Be simply loving, simply true.

RECORD

Coldest-ever day in May,
Daisies won't come out to play.
Still lovers play pull-and-push
Under the flame-flowered bush.

SONG: CARRICKFERGUS

Blackthorn flowers
Now in Carrickfergus
The blackthorn flowers
Ghostly pale
And I dream of you
Spring in Carrickfergus
Whoever hears me
I tell your tale

I see you there
Autumn Carrickfergus
You pick the sloeberry
Black as night
I still see you there
Black against the heavens
The blackthorn branches
Holding you so tight

Lovely Christmas
We were lost in Heaven
We drank our sloeberry
Gin and wine
And we laughed and cried
Winter Carrickfergus
Where nights are long
By your lover's side.

Come Eastertide
And the deathly flowers
Men good and true
Took her from my side
And they walled her in
Spring in Carrickfergus
Where stones are chilling
Where she paled and died

You fear woman
Men of Carrickfergus
You fear the she-devil
Casts her spell
Brews a witch's brew
For your sons and daughters
For Satan's trophies
In the halls of Hell

Men good and true
Men of Carrickfergus
Come Judgement Day
When we sinner's rise
You will see the sloe
That forbidden berry
Bitter night-black berry
In your very eyes

Blackthorn flowers
Home in Carrickfergus
The blackthorn flowers
Deathly pale
And I dream of you
Spring in Carrickfergus
Whoever hears me
I tell your tale

TWINS

Pain is the twin of pleasure—
One a sunny smile,
The other dark and secret, not
Welcome at the ball.

But they are true sisters.
Never come between.
They'll gobble you up, spit you out
And pick your bones clean.

Waltz with them till midnight—
Love them both to bits—
And have a brave face ready when
The glass slipper fits.

HAUNTED

Bring her back, for Heaven's sake!
She's fading into the past,
Looking a ghost, a reflection
In a cobwebbed pane of glass.

She's paler and blonder too.
She seems to be losing power.
Her eyes have gone weak, gas-fire blue—
Eyes that outblazed the cornflower.

LLANDAFF WALK

1. Pub

The Butcher's Arms, muscular and hairy.
He chops livers for lunch.
Like cats the lovers enter warily,
not daring to touch.

A sanctuary for men—quiet, early drinkers.
The lovers curl up by the fire.
The men turn away, sip from their puddles,
too polite to stare.

Now pools of women, rippling with giggles,
fill The Arms with sound;
the men start at sudden splashes of laughter,
either smile or frown.

Then quiet. The women exit merrily.
The lovers end lunch,
slip through The Arms and leave warily,
not daring to touch.

2. Garden

The Walled Garden has walls to keep out the God of Winds. It has no roof so as to let in the Gods of Sun and Rain. The lovers enter the Garden and find it crowded, all the benches occupied by people sunning themselves in the perfect summer weather. The lovers walk the path. They long for autumn and winter again, when they were foul-weather friends, the only humans here, the pigeons and squirrels on short rations, all the benches vacant and shining with wet, and the garden a lovely room with no roof where they could stand beneath the fig tree in the mizzle and touch and taste each other. They complete their circuit and leave the Garden, brush past the litter-basket Holy Well, and stroll down the hill.

3. Graveyard

Past the murder cottage
Where the Verger did his wife
(Electric fire in the bath
And down the drain for life)

The lovers walk the graveyard path—
No fear they will disturb
The slumber of the residents
Whose silence is superb.

A solitary raven perches
On an angel's locks.
He screeches `Nevermore!' and points
To graves filled by the pox.

He might as well demand those cherubs
Stop their kissing game.
Their marble ears hear `Evermore!'
All lovers are the same.

His name is Joy, the cherub boy—
The little girl is Hope.
Perhaps the Verger shall rise up
And wash their mouths with soap.

4. Tea Shop

This site may well be where a sacred well
Gave balm and zest to pagan penitents.
Here Christians built this cool Prebendal House,
And lively ladies of the W.I.
Serve tea and really splendid cakes and scones.

The lovers joke and natter with the ladies,
Then settle on the terrace to enjoy
Their tea and cake spiced with a silly question:
What can the `P.H.' on the teacups mean?
Maybe the words that rhyme with `cubic square'?

Right on cue the place fills up with schoolkids,
Huge and spotty, packed with rampant hormones.
The lovers flee, the ladies serving tea
Stop having fun to be grown-up and boring.

5. Cathedral

Disguised as tourists, the lovers
enter a place where they have no place.
A chill air of unwelcome seems
to envelop them as the door shuts;
they hold hands for a little warmth,
feeling disdain in the eye of
Celibate Ascending gazing upwards,
in the ascetic curl of his nostril.

Here is a place for warriors, though:
a spare wayside chapel listing
many exotic spots where lads
have died; the lovers know that sense
of being where you don't belong—
but how would it feel to die there?
A brace of clerics rattle off
some service, bang their books shut and scarper.

A place for the housewife, surely,
this Martyr's Chapel, shrine for all
down-on-the-knees doormat people.
Why else the votive Hoover left
standing on the scruffy, half-swept
carpet? The mild Martyr watches,
pityingly, from her window.
(At least, lovers, she knows where she belongs.)

Last, the Lady Chapel, perfect
for weddings, so pretty and
cheerful with its white Art Deco
Virgin and Child, its glittering
reredos in wood and gold leaf.
What a shame it makes the lovers
feel left out; I'm sure Our Lady
wouldn't want anyone to be excluded.

Still, maybe there is more in the
air than gouts of mouldy incense—
maybe change, and maybe even
change may have a human face:
Rossetti's triptych has been cleaned;
the Mother's face, still careworn and
troubled, seems more clearly the face
of a real woman, not some painted saint;

the Black Madonna has been given
her own niche; she dies facing her
Son, comforted by the mourning
first eleven, warmed by bright
terraces of candles which seem
always to light themselves as if
by magic, making you wonder.
The lovers light two candles, one for Joy
and one for Hope, and pray they will live on.

WELSH HARPIST

Like dalliant butterflies her hands
Flutter on the strings.
Her harp sings like a loving heart,
Full of tearful songs.

Now you, my darling, touch no strings—
No instrument to play—
Your lovely, loving, deft hands parted
From my singing body.

DEMON

The Demon has his purposes.
They are his own.
He tempts you with a real treat.
You turn it down.

So then he whispers in your ear:
Your love's untrue,
Your bladder's shot, the tax man
Is after you.

He doesn't care, or know a thing
Except a buck.
He's just a sad pleasure-pusher
Flogging his stock.

THANKSGIVING

`So now that I'm so fat,'
You ask me with a kiss,
`Can you still love all that?'

I gaze at so much bliss,
This you I do so love.
Is there some point I've missed?

Love, when push comes to shove,
The more of you there is,
The more there is to love.

IF ROSSETTI READ DICKINSON

Must parting be a part of Love—
Inevitable end?
With gaudy leaves and autumn sheaves
Descending the U-bend?

Does Love's Enemy lie out there,
Hunkering in the dusk,
Selling succulent, goblin fruit
That smells of mould and musk?

We gaze beyond the Sea of Death,
Conning for paradise,
Dreaming we'll be together there—
Palm trees and Pimm's on ice.

These metaphors we all live by,
They seem a touch naive.
Why wipe your tears and blow your nose,
Then blame it on your sleeve?

Our enemy, Christina dear,
Must surely lie in us?
`Ourself behind ourself,' she said—
Emily had it sussed.

NEARNESS

Lovers loathe impediment
Like convicts hate a key.
But take it away, they're terrified
To see no boundary.

Two naked, flayed bodies
Can barely bear to touch.
No barrier, no distance...
Nearness can be too much.

RELUCTANT DRAGON

Those travel agents flash their wares
In lurid signs of puce and mauve:
Barbados, Goa, Graz, Tangiers—
Choose where the fickle heart shall rove.

My heart can only choose to cling.
It will not wander foreign parts.
Such strange names have a lonely ring—
My heart must beat beside your heart.

`Well yes,' you say, `but darling, dear,
The cord that links our hearts is strong.
Please, don't be dull, don't summer here.
Our heart-string stretches hard and long.'

So now I write to you from Rome.
It's hot here. Lots of ruins too.
I ponder the Fall and coming home,
The properties of guts and yew.

See, my heart stretches, far enough
To find it will not break when bent,
That two hearts can be supple, tough
And true as the famed longbows of Gwent.

SONG: ROCK ON, CRIMSON CAVALIER

Chorus: Rock on, Crimson Cavalier
Steam on, Sierra Blue
Dream on, Golden Supernova
Dreams are always true

1. Crimson Cavalier, keep rocking
In the car park by the wildwood
Rock on, never stop

Walk on, girl with white Suzuki
Walk your chic designer sheep-dog
Try hard not to gawp

Chorus

2. Sierra Sapphire, keep on steaming
Windows shut and fogging over
Rock on, never stop

Bog off, man in black Range Rover
Standing stiffly in the lay-by
Eyes about to pop

Chorus

3. Burnt-out Nova in the beech wood
Do you dream of dancing lovers?
Dream on, let 'em bop

Dream you're Golden Supernova
Do the Samba on the green
Dream on and never stop

Chorus

VCR

This abandoned, idling video—
Like me and you?
Its blank, stammering treble zero
Brutally true?

What if we make it count again?
A hurtful thought,
But nothing like this hammering pain
Of flashing nought.

RIME OF ST MELANGELL

We celebrate the risen church
Of Melangell the fair,
Our gentle, fierce and loving saint
Who guards the hunted hare.

She halts the red-eyed, running dogs
With one dismissive frown.
They scent the hare but do not dare
To rend this lady's gown.

They mill around, poor sheepish hounds,
Lap at the laughing brook,
Then find some fascinating smell
To shun her dreaded look

And lope back to their kennels warm.
The furious hunter grips
His horn and finds it frozen fast
Onto his puckered lips.

`Who are you, lovely virgin witch?'
He cries when he can speak.
`Why charm my hounds and hunting horn?
Why spoil our hide-and-seek?'

`I am from far North,' she replies—
Her black eyes hold him tight—
`And weary of running, like the hare,
Hounded day and night,

Because I dared to spurn a man
My father bade me wed.
I chose another man myself
And took him to my bed.

Now he is dead and I am fled,
A homeless, hunted waif,
And when I found this hidden vale,
I prayed I might be safe.'

`I am a Welsh prince. Safe you are.
This land is mine by right.'
He tells himself he loves the witch,
But what he feels is fright.

`This land belongs to God,' she whispers,
`All his creatures share.
`Beware the sin of Pride,' she says,
`Be humble like the hare.'

`There are too many of the beasts,
They breed like flies in dung!'
He dares glance in her eyes again
And sees his body hung

Feet upwards from a blackened yew
Like so much strangled game.
He loves this lady; waves of terror
Flutter through his frame.

And then she lifts her muddied gown.
The hare from under creeps
To run and play another day.
And then the tall prince weeps.

And ever since this hidden vale
Has been her church and home,
And pilgrims have long ages come
For healing prayer and song.

One time the men of reason came,
Covered with blood and gore.
They broke her shrine, scattered her bones,
Unchained the dogs of war,

But now her place is whole again,
And pilgrims line the ways,
And experts come from far and near
To denigrate or praise.

We celebrate Saint Melangell
And bless her in our time.
We love the hare that hides within
And sing the ancient rhyme:

`He prayeth best who loveth best
All things both great and small.
For the dear God who loveth us
He made and loveth all.'

TIN MAN

I am the Tin Man now.
Beat on my chest. No heart.
Like banging on a bucket.
Where is my heart, my heart?
You said you took it home.

No place like home, you said,
There is no place like home.
Open it, take some blood,
And mix with spit and polish
To shine your Ruby Slippers.

Walk the Yellow Brick Road,
Find the Emerald City.
I am the Wizard now,
Scarecrow and Lion bow.
Heartless, I know no pity.

BOSOM BUDDY

The Goat of Guilt sits on my chest.
He grins and dribbles down his chin,
So that his drops of spittle form
A rank pool which reflects his grin.

He fixes me with devil eyes,
Then sighs, exhaling brimstone breath.
I am the Great White Weight, he whispers,
Your Bosom Buddy, unto death.

POETRY OR LOVE

Poetry is kaput.
Thank the stars above.
No more verse whingeing,
Certainty in love.

Poetry strikes back.
Schools of doubt swim in,
Followed by suspicion
Like a shark's fin.

Which will choose you?
Poetry, or Love?
Frantic fry and shark's snout,
Or wings like the dove?

CHRISTMAS TOY

I'll be your Tiny Ted
While we're apart,
Cuddly, breast-pocket rider,
Warm beside your heart.

And when you go to bed
Slip me in smart,
Your furry little hider,
In your warmest part.

MIRACLE

She died at thirty-seven,
The age she'd always said.
They buried her in all good faith,
In no doubt she was dead.

Talk about consternation.
She crashes the funeral feast—
No ghastly ghost but looking good
(Her skirt a little creased).

They're glad, of course, though pleasure
Falls short of prodigious.
It's awkward, like she's always been,
And vaguely sacriligious—

Seeing that resurrection
Is the province of Our Lord,
Who never blew the crowd a kiss
And shot off in a Ford.

So there she goes. That's that.
She did it for a thrill—
That's what they say—no Miracle's
Occurred, and never will.

THE MORE DECEIVED

The less deceived are those
Who know that life is short,
That wilt awaits the rose,
That missions all abort,

That death's the only truth,
And love ends in the sod.
So much for blinkered youth
Who think they're close to God.

But we are more deceived,
And many miles from youth,
So let us love, my love.
It's better than the truth.